Wiggling Earthworms

by Laura Hamilton Waxman

first step nonfiction

Lerner Publications ◆ Minneapolis

LERNER

e

SOURCE

Expand learning beyond the printed book. Download free, complementary educational resources for this book from our website, www.lerneresource.com.

The images in this book are used with the permission of: © iStockphoto.com/Mik122, pp. 4, 19; © iStockphoto.com/fiulo, p. 5; © D. Kucharski/ K. KucharskaShutterstock.com, p. 6; © mashe/Shutterstock.com, p. 7; © kurt_G/Shutterstock.com, p. 8; © iStockphoto.com/Alasdair Thomson, p. 9; © iStockphoto.com/MementoImage, p. 10; © iStockphoto.com/Dick Richter, p. 11; © iStockphoto.com/keckstein, p. 12; © Dennis, David M./Animals Animals, p. 13; © PHOTO FUN/Shutterstock.com, p. 14; © schankz/Shutterstock.com, pp. 15, 16, 18; © iStockphoto.com/Viorika, p. 17; © Alex Fieldhouse/Alamy, p. 20; © fiulo/iStock/Thinkstock, p. 21; © iStockphoto.com/bazilfoto, p. 22. Front cover: © iStockphoto.com/Mik122.

Main body text set in ITC Avant Garde Gothic Std Medium 21/25.
Typeface provided by International Typeface Corp.

Lerner Publications Company
A division of Lerner Publishing Group, Inc.
241 First Avenue North
Minneapolis, MN 55401 USA

For reading levels and more information, look up this title at www.lernerbooks.com.

Library of Congress Cataloging-in-Publication Data

Names: Waxman, Laura Hamilton, author.
Title: Wiggling earthworms / by Laura Hamilton Waxman.
Description: Minneapolis : Lerner Publications, [2016] | Series: First step nonfiction. Backyard critters | Audience: Ages 5–8. | Audience: K to grade 3. | Includes index.
Identifiers: LCCN 2015041870| ISBN 9781512408782 (lb : alk. paper) | ISBN 9781512412246 (pb : alk. paper)
Subjects: LCSH: Earthworms—Juvenile literature.
Classification: LCC QL391.A6 W39 2016 | DDC 592.64—dc23

LC record available at http://lccn.loc.gov/2015041870

Manufactured in the United States of America
1 – CG – 7/15/16

Table of Contents

Earthworm Bodies

Earthworms are soft and wiggly.

Their long bodies have no legs or feet.

Earthworms sense light with their skin.

Most earthworms have pink or brown skin.

Their bodies have many **segments**.

Earthworms have no eyes or ears.

A tiny mouth is at the front end.

The back end has a hole
for **waste**.

Where to Find Earthworms

Earthworms live in warm, wet dirt.

Some live under wet leaves
on the ground.

Some live in tunnels.

Earthworms often come above the ground when it rains.

Some **burrow** deep underground.

Earthworms eat mostly dead plants.

They find leaves and **roots**
in the dirt.

They also eat animal waste in **soil**.

Earthworms move by using their muscles to wiggle and stretch. 17

They leave their waste in
the dirt as they move.

Waste feeds plants so they can grow.

The waste makes the soil healthy for plants.

Roots need air and water to grow.

Earthworm tunnels bring air and water to the roots of plants.

Earthworms help our plants and gardens grow!

Earthworm Parts

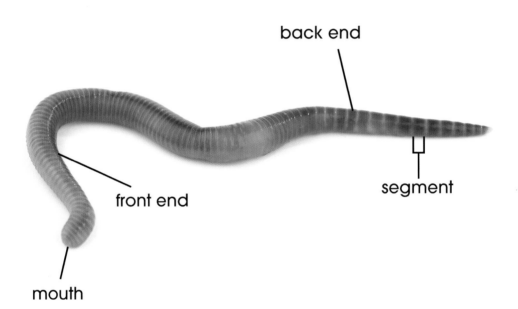

back end

segment

front end

mouth

Glossary

burrow – to tunnel or dig underneath something

roots – parts of plants that take in water and nutrients

segments – parts or sections

soil – black or brown dirt where plants can grow

waste – a substance that leaves an animal's body after it has eaten

Index